Building
Hong Kong

by Jan Morris

FormAsia

Building Hong Kong
©FormAsia Books Limited
Published by FormAsia Books Limited, 1995
Registered Address:
Caroline Centre, 10th Floor, 28 Yun Ping Road
Causeway Bay, Hong Kong
ISBN 962-7283-04-5

Written by Jan Morris
Text copyright © FormAsia Books Limited
Photographic Credits: All photographs are from The Stockhouse
Hong Kong with the exception of page 54 Gareth Jones;
70-89 FormAsia Books Limited;
116 Palmer & Turner; 120 Wong & Tung.
Designed by Ian Leung/Format Limited
Proofread by Geraldine Moor
Produced by Format Limited
Printed in Hong Kong by Leefung – Asco Printers Trading Limited

Building Hong Kong

*Like it or not, Hong Kong is one of the
most interesting cities mankind has ever created; and
as the feng shui geomancers have always said,
nothing is more auspicious for the
well-being of a people than the shape of
the city they inhabit.*

Red lacquered doors open onto a courtyard of the So Lau Yeun temple in Fanling. (Left) According to tradition, on the first day of Chinese New Year paper cutouts, couplets or wood-block prints of protective door gods are pasted on the entrance to family homesteads. (Previous pages) Roots of the indigenous Chinese banyan find a foothold in this century-old chiselled granite stairway of Island School.

Contents

Introduction

This book about the building of one of the world's great urban complexes is bound to have some sense of epitaph to it: for though the place is still irrepressibly building and rebuilding itself, these are the last years of the unique historical situation which have made Hong Kong what it is. For a century and a half east and west have met here in unexampled circumstances, sometimes in hostility, sometimes in collaboration, always in a relationship that has proved, for better or for worse, astonishingly fertile.

The west, originally in the guise of the British Empire, eventually expressing itself in the full furious panoply of international capitalism, has contributed technique, system, order and example; the east, which means in this context China, has provided insights, energies, ideas and a sense of underlying continuity. Sparks have flown from this conjunction as nowhere else: two elemental human forces have met here with a particular intimacy, in a few square miles of territory, and the effect has been colossal.

The Hong Kong which the book portrays stands at a moment of epitome. After 1997, when it returns from British rule to the sovereignty of China, and becomes the Special Administrative Region of Xianggang, it can never be the same again. Its momentum will doubtless be terrific still, but it will be a different momentum, obeying different rules and perhaps aimed at different objectives. Building Xianggang will have new meanings altogether. Hong Kong in the 1990s is the definitive Hong Kong; and whatever becomes of the place, whether it flourishes or founders, history will look back to the territory in its last British decade as a construction sui generis, never to be built again.

Jan Morris

Hong Kong is forever on the move; building, demolishing, redeveloping. Contractor's cranes atop Pacific Place, silhouetted against the morning sunrise. (Previous pages) Sir Aston Webb's Supreme Court building, now the Legislative Council, is the only remaining building of stature from an earlier era to grace Statue Square. (Following pages) Moss covered wall of an abandoned village at San Wai in the New Territories.

Preface

The only landmark on my horizon: two handsome baobab trees.

I grew up in one of the most isolated places on earth. On a tobacco farm near a little town in what was then South West Africa, now Namibia. It was empty of everything except space. And of that there was plenty. In every direction I cared to look, always only space. To this day I remember those wide empty plains as far as my eye could see. The limitless veld.

The only regular visitors to our farm was the local police force which would arrive on camel once a week on Saturdays, regular as clockwork, to make sure that all was well. Through the shimmer of the midday African heat with its accompanying red powdery dust, one could see them arriving two hours away, so flat and void was the countryside. I dreaded those visits. Invariably I would be lifted onto a grumbling camel as it was made to kneel and then have my picture taken. Regular as clockwork, every Saturday!

I must have been the most photographed child on the backs of camels in the entire world. That's how empty Namibia was. The only tangible inheritance I have from my mother are these childhood memories and photo albums filled with pages of faded pictures of me sitting on camels.

My closest friends on the adjacent tobacco farm were a two-hour jog away. Before I was obliged to attend "big" school in the town at the age of six, I would think nothing of wheeling my rusty bicycle rim in front of me to go and play on their ranch in the morning and return before sunset.

On the way the twisting, winding path — for in Africa no pathway is ever straight — would skirt the only landmark on my horizon: two handsome baobab trees.

Standing in awe beneath their majestic height, I would catch my breath and rest in their shade. It was the next best thing to being indoors; protected from the sun, from the rain, even from danger. Those were my first illusionary impressions of architecture. Of being within — what a small boy must have imagined tall buildings to be. They were the arrival hall of my young life. I loved those trees.

The baobabs acted also as town hall, church and even prison cell as on occasions I would stumble upon Herero elders seated beneath the trees in a circle on woven straw mats in an *ndaba*, or serious discussion, or festivities with statuesque turbaned women — and no Herero is under six feet tall — dancing separated from their menfolk, celebrating a marriage or the blessing of a birth. One evening I came across freshly spilled blood in the dry sand and an abandoned spear broken in two. Frightened, I raced home before darkness fell.

During those early years architecture expressed itself also in the form of liquid mud and cow dung. Mixed, it was the mortar filling between the branches which formed the ribs of the dwellings in which the servants lived. Recovering from illness or the acquisition of a fresh wife were festive occasions for the construction of a new home. Our resident farm mechanic, in leopard skins, shield, fangs and beer bottle tops tied around his ankles — instilled in me great reverence for he also doubled as the witch doctor — always performed a solo dance on these occasions, recited ancient verses punctuated with generous gulps of *shebeen* beer. Then with one well aimed swipe of his *assagai*, he would behead the family rooster before we were allowed to scoop the dung mixture with our bare hands and smear it smoothly on floor and walls, allowing the "mortar" to consolidate in the sun.

Faded, rambling and shuttered, the Huguenot family homestead.

It would seem to me almost inevitable, as if written in the grand scheme of things, that I should spend a great deal of my later life in an environment totally contrary to my isolated beginnings. In one of the most populous Asian cities on earth, so distantly removed from those boyhood dreams, yet still remain acutely conscious of space, either created or destructed around me. My open veld had now become isolated verdure islands languishing in the South China Sea. The cluster of straw and mud huts from my mother's farm with their distinctive patterned walls had become the abandoned Hakka villages and gabled ancestral homes topped with glazed porcelain gargoyles and gods dreaming in the dragon hills of Kowloon. The faded dignity of a less hurried era of the China Trade, its granite and colonnaded façades, symbol of a now retreating empire, are tangible links with my Huguenot family homestead, also faded, rambling and shuttered with its wide verandah, to keep at bay the African heat. My handsome baobab trees are transformed into ever taller and perplexingly elegant skyscrapers constructed in steel and cobalt glass on Hong Kong's waterfront or around Statue Square, the heart of the city. The family witch doctor cum mechanic now wears the mandarin gown of a practicing Taoist geomancer; flutters a fan, recites snatches from the Chinese classics and consults his feng shui compass as he divines the auspicious well being of a people and the shape of the city they inhabit as its destiny hurtles towards an uncertain future soon to be governed by a new landlord.

Frank Fischbeck, *FormAsia Books*

The Finest Sight in Asia

Sunrise over the harbour, with Central's cityscape now dominated by the seventy-storey Bank of China Tower. (Left) To Britain's Lord Palmerston, it was a "barren rock" that would never become a significant mart of trade. To Lord Napier, it was a "safe and commodious harbour." To the merchants involved in the 19th-century China Trade, Hong Kong presented an irresistible challenge. (Previous pages) The bumpy blue ridge of the hills to the east perfectly sets off the archipelago.

I f nobody had erected so much as a hut or a hovel in the territory called Hong Kong, people would still come to look at the place for the splendour of its setting. A little to the east of the Pearl River estuary, the great waterway which gives access to Guangzhou (old Canton) and the interior of southern China, an archipelago lies scattered off the coast. Collectively its islands were once called the Ladrones, the Pirate Islands, and in some lights they do have a lurking, watchful quality. At other times, though, when the sea is the vivid greenish-blue so common in Chinese waters, when the humped shapes of the islands, seen against the sun, seem to have acquired a radiance of their own, they sometimes suggest to me those islets of legend which tantalizingly come and go, or are visible only if one stands upon a magic stone.

21

The mainland shore is mountainous here, and the bumpy blue ridge of the hills to the east, running down to a brief coastal plain, perfectly sets off the archipelago. A superb natural harbour is formed by the conjunction, and with the distant shimmer of the estuary to the south, the long line of China running away to the north, it is as though the whole scene has been devised by some genius landscape architect. Not only is it lovely, but it seems just made for consequence. Economically, as it happens, its situation is unpromising, Guangzhou itself being much better placed as a port. The seductive power of the setting, though, makes one feel that however the course of history had run, sooner or later a great city would inevitably have arisen upon the shores of Hong Kong.

As it is, a city stands there with a vengeance. Historical circumstance brought the British Empire here, and in the final decade of the 20th century the Crown Colony of Hong Kong still extends all around that harbour; on Hong Kong Island itself and on several other islands of the archipelago, all over the neighbouring coastal plain of Kowloon, beyond and around the mountains in the country called the New Territories. It is in effect a city-state of six million people, and though statistically most of its land remains undeveloped hill country, its impact is essentially urban. Perhaps nowhere else on earth illustrates so dramatically the nature of the city, because unlike other great metropoles Hong Kong has something inorganically sudden about it, something explosive, so artificial is the reason for its existence, so brutal the contrast between its presence there and that celestially timeless background.

Energy Materialized

For my own tastes it offers the finest sight in Asia. Seen as a whole, without detail, from some high point of the islands — from Victoria Peak, say, which forms the apex of Hong Kong Island — the city looks a stupendous unity. Its predominant colour is white, set against the green of the hills and the green-blue of the water, and for a huge industrial complex its air is surprisingly clear. This gives a peculiar excitement to its overwhelming suggestion of energy.

For it really looks, from such a vantage point, like energy materialized. The harbour is full of ships, line upon line of moored ships stretching away towards the outer anchorages, freighters perpetually coming and going, cruise ships and warships very often, junks and sampans and launches and ferries and hydrofoils and even an occasional yacht tacking precariously through the traffic. Every few moments, it seems, a jet lumbers into the sky from the runway at the harbour's edge, and wherever one looks endless streams of vehicles are pressing their way inexorably along streets, up hills, over flyovers, in and out of tunnels, as though they are not self-propelled at all, but are simply civic molecules.

Hardly less dynamic is the structure of Hong Kong, the mass of masonry, steel and glass which now surrounds the harbour. It is an essentially restless structure. It seems to be almost moving before one's eyes. It sprouts in thickets, clusters, sudden spikes. It is jam-packed on the flat ground, so tightly that often there hardly seem to be streets between the buildings; it climbs up the hill slopes in jagged outcrops; it presses along the waterfront, on the mainland and on the island shore, in serried slabs of glass, steel and concrete. It flashes, too, with the glint of sunlight on its windows, with blinking lights, with the bright movement of cars, ships and aircraft, and this gives it an extra air of inner compulsion, like a reactor.

In short, if the purpose of architecture is to express function, Hong Kong has got it right. This place lives by commercial and financial excitement, and so it most certainly appears. That it also contrives to look astonishingly beautiful, at least from a distance, says something about the nature of aesthetics; for if Hong Kong's beauty is partly the objective beauty of its environment, it is partly the subjective beauty of its own intentions — the allure of capitalist enterprise, competition and greed, translated into magnificent spectacle. Whatever else one might say about the building of Hong Kong, one could never call it dull.

A Not Very Important Corner of The Manchu Empire

I t has all happened, in effect, in two centuries. Very few structures there are any older than that. Until the British seized Hong Kong Island in 1841, this place was a not very important corner of the Manchu Empire, a sovereignty which believed itself divinely supreme among all the kingdoms of the earth. The territory was strategically and economically unimportant, and it possessed nothing remotely approaching a city.

Traditional insular villages, walled or moated, were characteristic of the clans who farmed the valleys of the Dragon Hills in the New Territories. (Left) Glazed porcelain tiles from the kilns of Shekwan, near Canton, grace the roof of the Wong Tai Sin temple in Kowloon.

The Chinese certainly called their local administrative centre Kowloon City, but it was really no more than a small walled town on the peninsula. Here and there through the territory they built a few forts and official outposts, but for the most part the indigenes were allowed to run their own affairs. This they did with elaborate systems but with varying degrees of serenity, since they were frequently at odds with one another. They were of several Chinese races, many of them lived on board junks and sampans, and they were dominated by five Cantonese clans, each controlling its own fortified villages, lands and even armies. It was a sophisticated society in some ways, governed by well-defined rules of protocol and inheritance; and it was given a mystic visual unity by the laws of feng shui, "wind and water", the ancient Chinese geomancy of placement which governed the positioning of everything, from tombs to farms to thickets.

Ambiguous Composures

Physically not much is left of that old society. Roads and railways, sprawling suburbs, the decline of agriculture, the vast growth of populations — all these have swamped it, and have left its surviving structures as rare anomalies. On the hills, however, which are still largely uninhabited, often one discerns the omega-shaped graves in which the bones of the dead lie, their sites meticulously calculated by the geomancers; and somehow they are so perfectly placed there, they look so proper against the mountain contours, that they seem to project unaccustomed circuits of calm over the frenzied scenes below.

Similarly the remaining buildings of Manchu Hong Kong, though they are not always particularly handsome, often retain an ambiguous composure. Many of them are Taoist temples, and these in particular seem marvellously impervious to commotion. The temple of the sea-goddess Tin Hau at Joss House Bay, for example, stands on a site recognized as particularly favourable at least since the 13th century, and though at weekends and on festival days it is overrun by thousands of visitors, it still manages to feel almost arcanely detached above its bay. Even more remarkably insulated is the most famous Hong Kong holy place of them all, the Man Mo temple on Hollywood Road in the heart of Central's business district. Cacophonous with drums and bells, gaudy with crimson banners, murky with incense, thick with tourists, attended by beggars, surrounded by tumultuous traffic, even

The Tsui Shing Lau pagoda, though secular in character, originally had seven storeys. The upper four floors were destroyed by a typhoon. The present structure, still standing, is about two hundred years old. (Previous pages) The now faded, abandoned Man Shek Tong ancestral halls, once handsomely crafted with timber and granite, were pivotal to village life of the Tang clan.

so it remains to my mind unmistakably blessed; for amidst the indescribable urban congestion it still stands, as its heritage demands, gracefully in the lee of a hill, looking down towards water.

There are several hundred such Manchu temples in Hong Kong, dedicated to many divinities, ranging in size from mere shrines to substantial places of worship and divination. Most of them follow the same basic ground plan — three halls leading one into another; built of stone, brick and wood; architecturally in almost all the roof line is important — that symbol-encrusted ridge, all dragons, divinities and folk emblems, which represents to most of us the very essence of Chinese design.

Memories Overwhelmed

Secular remains of the Manchu Empire are harder to find. A dozen or so walled villages, some of them dilapidated and most of them hemmed in by urbanization, are the chief memorials to its old social systems. Nobody will ever build such villages again, for they reflect a way of life that can never recur — powerfully clan-dominated communities, sharing possession of the land, cap-a-pie against enemies and politically semiautonomous. They had their temples, their study halls which were places of local learning, their ancestral halls devoted to the souls of the departed. The best known of them, Kat Hing Wai in the New Territories, is built of dour grey brick to an uncompromising grid system, with the remains of a moat around it, square corner towers and a forbidding gateway; it is inhabited by members of the Tang clan, as it has been for several centuries, but stands immediately beside a busy highway, and has long been defiled by tourism.

More evocative is the village of Tsang Tai Uk, which is slightly further off the beaten track, and less demanding of a character. It reminds me rather of a medieval castle community somewhere in Italy. Tucked away beside the northern entrance to the Lion Rock tunnel, which pierces the Kowloon hills, it remains hauntingly suggestive of ancient values. From the outside it appears to be one large building, gable-ended and high-walled, but it is really a well-ordered congeries of separate dwellings. In the heart of it stands its temple, and within its surrounding walls four parallel brick alleys, littered nowadays with bicycles, washing machines, dogs and babies,

Reflecting the past glory of the Imperial City in Peking, weather-worn glazed roof tiles of the Po Lin Monastery — high in the hills of Lantau Island — begin to show their age. (Previous pages) The silhouette of a Hakka villager in her distinctive wide-brimmed hat is glimpsed through a doorway of her now derelict home. Only the elderly remain in their abandoned villages. (Following pages) In Manchu, temples and study halls, the symbol-encrusted roof of dragons, divinities and folk figures in wood or glazed porcelain served functions both structural and ornamental.

giving the impression still of an extended family residence, rooted and self-contained.

Outside the walled villages not many private homes survive from pre-colonial Hong Kong, and those that do are generally tumbledown, or have been so extended and modernized as to be almost unrecognizable as Manchu structures at all — only occasionally in the remoter valleys, as one flies over the hills in a helicopter, does one see an ancient farmstead, or a group of cottages, that looks unchanged since the Middle Ages. Here and there, however, there are traces of the imperial organization which, from its distant headquarters in Beijing, imposed its authority upon this countryside. On the island of Lantau stands the imposing walls of one of the Celestial Government's outlying naval bases: venerable guns still stand upon its ramparts, facing the sea where the war junks anchored, and within the courtyard an infants' school occupies in merry anomaly the promenade where the Emperor's admirals swaggered. And well into the 1990s there survived on its original site a vestigial relic of the Imperial Yamen itself, the administrative office within the walls of Kowloon City from which Manchu Hong Kong was theoretically governed.

Long ago Kowloon City found itself surrounded by the hive-like mass of modern Kowloon, parts of which are the most densely populated places on the earth's surface. The walls of the old imperial town were torn down, and almost nothing was left of its structure. Like a ghost, though, there remained a quarter known spectrally as the Walled City of Kowloon — a notoriously awful and dangerous slum of high tenements, riddled with dark alleys like rat runs, impenetrable to wheeled traffic and of such doubtful legal status that for years it was the haunt of thieves, drug dealers and illegal practitioners of every calling. It is there no longer, for they have pulled it down at last in the interests of hygiene and modernity, but to the end there was still to be found, deep in the noisome depths of it, an ancient stone building with a wooden roof which was once the seat of the imperial magistracy — all but lost in the jumble of it all, just as the authority of the Manchus themselves, here as everywhere else in their once vast dominions, is only a memory overwhelmed.

41

Bamboo and Geomancy

If the power of the Manchus has gone, like most of their structures, their methods and philosophies still tenaciously influence the building of Hong Kong. This is one of the most mercilessly modern cities on earth, yet it builds its buildings in ways that would not seem altogether alien to the mandarins of the old Empire. The minute the construction workers arrive upon a site, they are likely to put up just the kind of temporary shelters, wooden stakes crowned with a roof of matting, that the peasants of old China erected in Manchu times; as if to say, this is the way we always did it, this is the way we mean to go on.

Scaffolders, who usually work in teams of three, erect a bamboo framework on a waterfront construction site. (Left) Clusters of uncut bamboo used as scaffolding in the building industry.

And when the new skyscraper goes up above, to be equipped with every last device of electronic and engineering technique, the scaffolding that supports its towering structure, rising floor by floor with almost unnatural speed, is made not of steel or alloy, but of thousands upon thousands of bamboo rods, lashed together with reed cords. It looks like a vast wooden web, within which the construction elevators rise and fall, the hard-hat builders clamber and the huge shining thing of steel and glass, marble and aluminium, mysteriously takes shape. Every stranger is astonished by this spectacle, and by the sight of the scaffolders, sheaves of reed-lashings dangling from their belts, insouciantly balancing their way along dizzy struts to raise the web another storey. In Hong Kong, though, it is a familiar scene of daily life, inescapable and unchanging. It is also a kind of declaration.

For while those scaffoldings speak unmistakably of the Chinese genius for adaptability or even serendipity — the eager use of whatever is to hand, whether for building or eating or curing ailments — they also refer to something profounder: the Chinese sense of the organic. Even now the building art in Hong Kong feels to me anomalously close to the soil, retaining an almost atavistic affinity with its materials. Brick, marble and wood of all sorts respond naturally to these builders' hands. To my susceptible eye even frameworks of steel and concrete somehow seem truer and simpler than they do elsewhere, and everything is given a symbolic sponsorship by those original cradles of bamboo.

Bamboo! It is Chineseness in Essence

Clumps of it stand in graceful decoration at the edges of Chinese art (as in the leviathan mural which embellishes twenty floors of the Island Shangri-la Hotel, and is said to be the largest ever painted). It has provided the pulp for great works of literature. It makes exquisite furniture and serviceable rafts. Pet birds chirp through bars of it. Musicians play upon its flutes. Its leaves make hats and cloaks. You can cook fish inside it, or eat its roots, or take its pith as medicine.

One of a pair of granite Chinese lions guarding the entrance of the Tin Hau temple on Cheung Chau Island. (Previous pages) A sign writer locks himself securely around supporting bamboo to paint the final touches to a real estate hoarding.

And every day of every year, up it goes in its intricate patterns to bring another new Hong Kong building into the world.

All this reminds me of Venice, whose palaces are supported by forests of wooden pilings in the mud, and whose loftiest splendours depended always upon the diligence of craftsmen and the dictates of inherited custom. Just as Venice remains for ever a memorial to the craft guilds of the Renaissance, so Hong Kong, this terrific exhibition of cosmopolitan modernism, anomalously perpetuates many an ancient Chinese skill and conviction. Opulence itself, the leitmotiv of Hong Kong architecture, is expressed here in manners that would be familiar to the creators of the Forbidden City in Beijing: in the exquisite putting together of marble or granite, in elaborate woodwork and enormous murals, in statuary of monumental proportions and landscaping full of symbolism.

Buddhist and Taoist temples are still being built in Hong Kong, to the old patterns and in the old style. Po Lin, the famous Buddhist temple on Lantau Island, looks immemorial with its ochre-tiled roofs, wide eaves and marble terraces, but mostly dates from the 1970s. The great Taoist temple of Wong Tai Sin, which was opened in 1973, is a startling contemporary incarnation of traditional temple architecture: its design is true to ancient precedent, much of its building materials came from quarries in China which have supplied temples for centuries, and in its flanks proliferate the stalls of the soothsayers, the palmists and the sellers of joss sticks, but it stands in the heart of an immense modern development of high-rise blocks, expressways and flyovers. There is a splendid modern pagoda at the Temple of the Thousand Buddhas at Sha Tin in the New Territories (itself not very old — its founder died only in 1965, and is now preserved there in a glass case).

Chinese millionaires of Hong Kong still commission mansions rich in the crimson decoration of old China, and guarded by curled stone beasts. Boat builders construct fishing boats and pleasure craft recognizably descended from the junks and sampans of ancient times,

The world's largest outdoor bronze Buddha on Lantau Island is thirty-three metres tall, weighs two hundred and fifty tonnes and was constructed by the China Astronomical Industry Scientific and Consultative Corporation, manufacturers of rockets and satellites. (Previous pages) Bamboo latticework engulfs the interior of the century-old Catholic Cathedral of Immaculate Conception in preparation for craftsmen to refurbish the walls and ceiling. (Following pages) A veritable curtain of bamboo; the ingenious maze of scaffolding forms the basis of a makeshift opera house in preparation for Chinese New Year festivities.

with their powerfully rounded bows and high poops. The Tsuen Wan Columbarium, built in the 1980s, is a high-rise cemetery for the storage of ancestral ashes, watched over as tradition decrees by "chasers-away of evil" — stone Chimerae with dragon heads, phoenix wings, lion bodies and tiger tails.

The bronze lions that stand outside the spectacularly contemporary Hongkong and Shanghai Bank headquarters were inherited from the bank's earlier premises; but they too trace their meaning back to the protective animal images of medieval China, and to this day their paws are stroked by passers-by hoping for good luck. The little water garden that attends the mighty Bank of China skyscraper is a deliberate echo of the lake-rock-and-bridge motif so inescapable in traditional Chinese landscaping. High on Lantau, beside Po Lin, often mist-shrouded or half lost in drizzle, there recently went up the largest image of the Buddha ever created: it was made by the China Astronomical Industry Scientific and Consultative Corporation, manufacturers of rockets and satellites, but looming there so grandly above its monastery it already seems as timeless as China itself.

The wall itself, the basic structure of architecture, often has extra significance here. Of course a Hong Kong wall can sustain or define a structure, but it can also have metaphysical meanings, as a protection against the hostile spirit world, and as a repository of human strength — as recently as the 1960s, when the Plover Dam was being built in the New Territories, it was widely rumoured that live children were to be buried within its foundations. And when a Hong Kong building is completed, however advanced its architecture and secular its functions, it is likely to be opened with a ceremonial lion dance, designed to keep the demons away for good, and propitiate all the gods of wealth.

57

Feng Shui:
Balancing the Elements

Hong Kong's feng shui men (there are few, if any, women) have generally succeeded their fathers in the calling. (Left) Eminent geomancers whose expertise is partly philosophical, partly mathematical are respected men in their communities.

Underlying all the building of Hong Kong, as the Christian ethic sustained the spirit of Venice, is Confucianism, the philosophy that has transcended all the religions and ideologies, all the Empires and Republics of China. Feng shui is Confucian thinking applied to the building art, and is intended to bring to the construction of temples, houses, offices and cities the same balance of the elements, the proper combination of yin and yang, that should govern life itself. In a Hong Kong dedicated to the making of money, the display of wealth and all the shibboleths of material progress, it is immensely potent still.

Every bump and juncture of terrain affects feng shui, which makes it a complicated influence upon constructions of all kinds. A building must not be so sited as to interfere with the *chi*, the breath of the universe, and it must harmonize with all the shapes and forces of nature. The best possible site for a building is said to be between two spurs of hillside sloping down towards water; failing that, the builder must do his best not to clash with the dispositions of nature, preferably by hiring a professional geomancer (easy to find in Hong Kong still) to advise him with the help of his mystic instruments and his specialized training.

In general these theories of natural science amount to an arcane form of environmental planning; in the detail, with their undertones of animism and masonic suggestion, they add peculiar subtleties to the practice of building in Hong Kong. Always over the shoulder of the builder, the architect or the patron stands the geomancer, in the popular mind at least as important a figure. Hong Kong's feng shui men (there are few, if any, women) have generally succeeded their fathers in the calling, some inheriting from their forebears the traditional knowledge of ancient feng shui schools with China. They come in all kinds, from the simplest to the most sophisticated. At one end, village geomancers of the New Territories can be more or less indistinguishable from wizards; at the other, there stand educated professional men whose expertise is partly philosophical, partly mathematical, and who are important men in their communities — rich too, for the best geomancy does not come cheap.

Belief in Feng Shui

The popular belief in feng shui, and in the dangers of ignoring it, is ineradicable. Chinese people will go to great lengths and expense to avoid bad feng shui, in life as in death; for example, spending large sums of money in consulting geomancers as to propitious places for family graves — often, as it turns out, in fearfully inaccessible locations on distant slopes above the sea. Many Europeans in Hong Kong, too, half believe in feng shui, regarding it as a persuasive example of folk wisdom, a valuable system of aesthetic control, or at worst an entertaining superstition one might just as well humour.

This means that feng shui plays its part in every aspect of Hong Kong building, from corporate headquarters to tenement, and curiously influences the architecture of the place. Hong Kong law does not allow a citizen to bring an action if his own feng shui has been ruined by the erection of a neighbouring building, but the government has often paid compensation to people who feel their mystic well-being has been wrecked by a new road or dam. If only to keep his neighbours and employees happy, the most sceptical developer dare not commission a building without consulting a feng shui practitioner concerning the axis of its construction, the most propitious pitch of its staircases or the proper arrangement of its entrances (through which, if skilled care is not taken, evil influences may circulate with the air conditioning).

Eminent geomancers are often honoured guests at the opening of vast new structures to which they have applied their knowledge, and Hong Kong lore is full of anecdotes about their influence, some more reliable than others. A power station has been given an extra and unnecessary chimney because of feng shui. The escalators of an office block have been resited for more propitious effect. The doors of a luxury hotel would be placed altogether differently, were it not for the advice of the feng shui man. The underground line of the Mass Transit Railway was repeatedly shifted for the sake of feng shui. Only the demands of feng shui, it is often said, have kept Statue Square, in the heart of the financial district, free of obstructive building; and everybody knows that in the years before the British withdrawal the feng shui of Government House, once ideal, has been fatefully ruined by the emergence of enormous office blocks all around it.

So, in a city where the past often seems disposable, or for that matter already disposed, immemorial ideas and techniques live on. They make the building of Hong Kong a far less mechanistic process than it may appear; they link this archetypal city of the late 20th century with its vicarious roots far away in time and space; they bring to the electronic age some memories of the age of craftsmanship; and they are embodied almost mystical. I sometimes think, in those intricate meshes of bamboo scaffolding, out of which every new skyscraper emerges as from a chrysalis.

A Classic Outpost of British Imperialism

The first permanent building the British built, when they stepped ashore at Possession Point, Hong Kong Island, in 1841, was very properly an opium warehouse; trade was their purpose, opium their prime commodity of the day. The first residential building was a bungalow built for himself by James Matheson, a partner in the leading British merchant enterprise, with a veranda around it and its own plantation of coconuts; it was scathingly described as being "half New South Wales, half native production", and its trees soon wilted in Hong Kong's distinctly uncoconut climate.

The Supreme Court, completed in 1905 under the supervision of Sir Aston Webb, architect of the Victoria and Albert Museum in London. (Left) Arched and balustraded verandas in the prestigious waterfront headquarters of the China Trade.

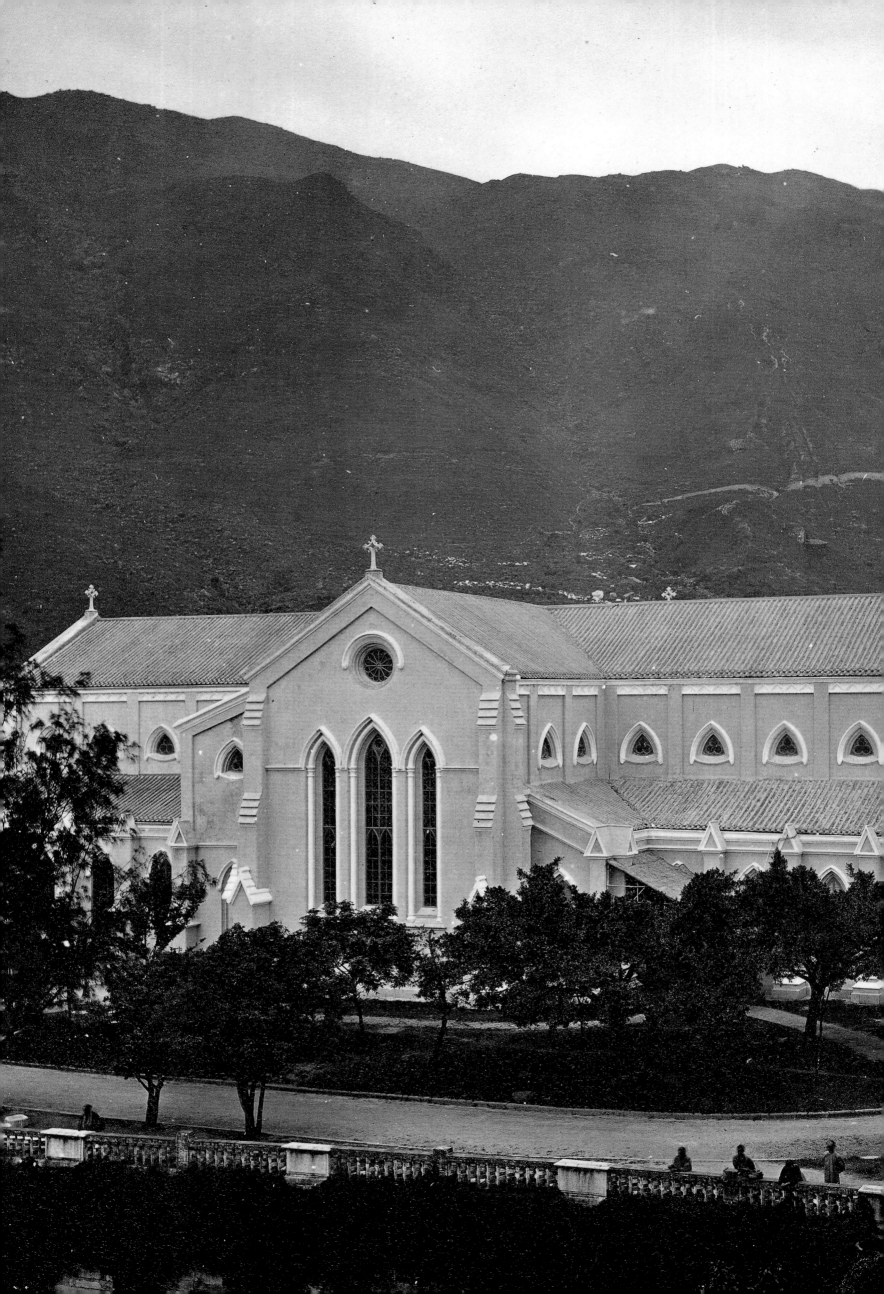

Neither building survives, neither was very memorable, but they were the beginning of great things. The population of Hong Kong would always remain overwhelmingly Chinese, but by the early 20th century the British, having acquired the Kowloon Peninsula in 1860, the New Territories in 1898, had created upon this foreshore an impressive mercantile city in their own imperial mould.

This was not achieved all at once. For a large part of the Victorian century British Hong Kong had rather a Mediterranean look, partly because of the influence of the Portuguese, who had occupied their nearby territory of Macao since the 16th century. The main commercial and administrative settlement, on the north shore of Hong Kong Island, was indeed called Victoria, but visitors sometimes likened it to Genoa, and pictures from the 1850s and 1860s certainly do not make it look very British. It had its Government House, of course, and its Anglican cathedral, and its barracks, and its club; but the general architectural tone of it was set by the arches and porticoed Italianate buildings which lined the waterfront, three or four storeys high, sometimes with small domes or cupolas, and almost always with open verandas. A few hundred yards each way along the shore the town petered out into a muddle of Chinese huts, bamboo and matting sheds and warehouses; the life of the colony was conducted within the mesh of a few short semitropical streets, dusty or muddy according to the season, and all looking down to the waterfront, the *raison d'être* of it all, where the company tenders stood at their piers, or hung from davits all along the quay. If the town had a centre, it was the Pedder Street boat landing, with a clock tower which acted both as a civic symbol and a navigational beacon.

Almost nothing is left of this small colonial seaport, which was not generally admired, which had a reputation for the raffish and the scandalous, and which certainly disregarded all the precepts of the geomancers. The cathedral is still there, though enlarged over the years; Government House is on the same site, though repeatedly aggrandized; a few segments of mid-Victorian barrack blocks survive, converted to other uses and barely recognizable. For the rest, almost

(*Previous pages*) *Queen's Road through the commercial heart of Hong Kong was a refined thoroughfare. However, it became more colourful as it snaked through the Chinese section of town (left) between open fronted shops, overcrowded tenements and impromptu markets.*

all one can find is an occasional crumbled portico, a broken jalousie, or a forlornly overgrown garden awaiting imminent development. Early colonial Hong Kong is hardly more than a sepia allusion, and this is because in the later years of the 19th century, and in the first part of the 20th, the colony was transformed into a classic outpost of British imperialism, and achieved indeed a transient architectural dignity.

Pearl of the Orient

The acquisition first of the Kowloon peninsula, then of the land behind it, meant that Hong Kong became a twin city of the harbour. The centre of things remained the waterfront of Victoria, now more generally known as Central, but more and more activity, social and commercial, moved to Kowloon side. The harbour was integrated, as it were, into the city, and by the heady years of *fin de siècle*, the climactic years of British imperialism, Hong Kong had acquired a finished look. By then Kowloon had become the railhead of the Canton railway, linked with tracks all across Asia to western Europe, and Hong Kong was on the routes of many of the world's shipping lines. It was an essential and familiar station of imperial communications — a link, as Lord Curzon the imperialist romantically put it, "in that great chain of fortresses which from Spain to China girdles half the globe."

Of course, it still all looked to the waterfront. By now indeed it looked down from the high contours of Victoria Peak, where a hill station had been established in the classic colonial manner, with bridle paths, arboured villas, a church, a club, and a boldly precipitous funicular railway (British built, of course) linking it with the harbour below. This had become, by then, virtually a civic highway itself, for the steam ferries that crossed it regular as clockwork brought the new urban districts of Kowloon within a few minutes of Central, and meant that large, new middle-class residential quarters had developed over there, too.

The Easternmost Possession

The heart and emblem of it, nevertheless, remained the Central waterfront. In Hong Kong at the turn of the century, only some six thousand Europeans lived among two hundred thousand Chinese, but you would hardly have guessed it from the visual impact of the place, as you sailed into its harbour from a P & O liner, say, or stepped from your sleeper at the Kowloon railway station. Economically the colony had never quite fulfiled itself, its fortunes having proved uncomfortably volatile, but its presence was undeniably majestic. Imperial propagandists loved it, and called it The Easternmost Possession, or Britain's Pearl of the Orient.

Much of Central was built on land reclaimed from the sea, in successive profitable stages. This had allowed the construction of an esplanade along much of the waterfront, and in the middle of this fine boulevard stood a true civic focus, a plaza, open to the harbour at its northern side. It was a sea plaza, so to speak, bringing the meaning of the harbour into the very heart of the city. It was like the Piazza Grande at Trieste, the seaport of the Austria-Hungarian Empire, which opened emblematically upon the Adriatic; or like Lisbon's majestic Praca do Comércio, looking out to the Portuguese sea routes — its inspiration, perhaps, for architecturally the influence of Macao was still active in Hong Kong.

The Pedder Street clock tower had been demolished, and this grand square was now the focus of everything. It was first called Royal Square, later Statue Square. Queen Victoria herself stood in effigy beneath a cupola in the centre of it, and she was joined over the years by many other sculpted worthies, mostly royal, and surrounded by buildings hardly less institutional. There was, for instance, the headquarters of the Hongkong and Shanghai Bank, the most powerful financial institution of the colony, and one of the most important in the east: a stately domed building part classical, part Gothic, altogether imperial. There was the Hong Kong Club, the prime social

institution, large, square and complacent, with a cricket ground behind. There was the Supreme Court, the ultimate legal institution of the place, completed in 1905 under the supervision of Sir Aston Webb, architect of the Victoria and Albert Museum in London — a handsome domed structure with arcades around it and a noble first-floor gallery.

All in all, Statue Square was a place of balanced consequence, presiding figuratively, as well as physically, over the ceaseless bustle of the harbour before it. Around it, and across the water, the late Victorians built a plethora of buildings in their best imperial manner. There was a towered University and a French classical City Hall and a Royal Observatory on a hill. A ballroom was appended to Government House. The great merchant firms built themselves heavy headquarters, sometimes in Gothic, sometimes in classical modes, and sometimes in the eclectically Indianified kind known as Indo-Saracenic. The streets behind the waterfront, their potholes and banyans gone, were now extremely solid commercial thoroughfares, given exoticism only by the myriad Chinese, the turbaned Sikh doormen, the palanquins and the rickshaws that moved through them.

Hong Kong had come into its architectural own, and appeared both complete and permanent. The 1920s and 1930s seemed only to seal the ensemble; Hong Kong's principal new buildings of the inter-war period were a grandiose hotel, The Peninsula, opposite the railway station in Kowloon, and a new headquarters for the Hongkong and Shanghai Bank which was claimed to be the tallest structure between California and Egypt (the Great Pyramid was twice as tall). It all seemed grand and proper, the Pax Britannica in masonry; but all too soon, under the impact of World War II, when the Japanese humiliatingly occupied the colony, the decline of the imperial conviction and the emergence of Communist China, the Hong Kong of *fin de siècle* was to prove itself not so absolute after all.

Muddle and Rebirth

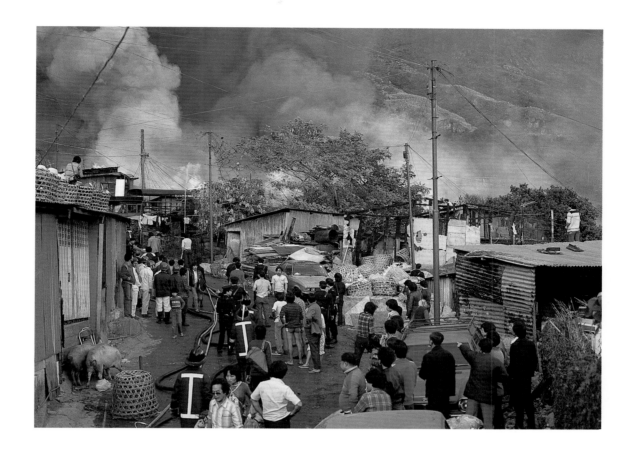

Two great historical progressions brought rebirth to Hong Kong. The first was the industrialization of the territory, which made of it in the years after World War II not merely a seaport and exchange, but an immense manufacturing centre. The second was the liberalization, in its declining years, of the British Empire. From the start Hong Kong had existed in reflex to its overwhelming neighbour, China. The Communist revolution there, in 1949, exiled into the colony, among several hundred thousand refugees, scores of brilliantly inventive Chinese industrialists, mostly from Shanghai. Almost at the same time the Korean War led to an embargo on trade with Communist China, obliging the old entrepôt Hong Kong to find other ways of making a living. The colony turned to making things, and in no time at all it had become one of the world's chief centres of manufacturing industry. A furious architectural muddle was the consequence.

(Previous pages) Dense high-rise clusters of thirty-five-storey buildings mark the centre of City One in Sha Tin. These estates, like South Horizon in Ap Lei Chow (left), are basic to the architectural effect of Hong Kong. Most modern housing complexes are attended by gardens, swimming pools, schools, cinemas and shopping plazas.

Very little planning control governed the explosive expansion of the city, and its predominant style was one of inchoate modernism. Hardly a building of Hong Kong's period of industrialization, between the 1950s and the 1980s, was very memorable. Thirty years after World War II, though the sheer scale of development made Hong Kong visually more exciting than ever, architecturally it was sadly arid.

Then something happened to make Hong Kong a place of interest, if not at first to architectural critics, at least to town planners throughout the world. By tradition Hong Kong social planning was almost a contradiction in terms, so dedicated had the colony always been to laissez faire in every aspect of public or private life. Times changed, however. Even in Hong Kong social planning became ideologically acceptable, and over the next decades the colony's government was to become perhaps the most socially interventionist the empire had ever known. On Christmas Eve in 1953, fifty thousand of those people were made homeless by a fire in Kowloon. The government embarked upon a building project of almost theatrical innovation, destined to change not just the look of Hong Kong, but its very character.

Hong Kong then was still largely a city of refugees. Fired by the disaster of the fire, the government now set out to house them all in vast public housing schemes, and more particularly in a series of new towns.

It was one of the most ambitious state housing developments in history; within thirty years about as many people lived in the New Territories as lived in the original urban settlements.

Today they are basic to the architectural effect of Hong Kong. If they look sterile at first in their concrete functionalism, soon their inhabitants turn them into very exhibitions of human virility: small businesses flourish on every corner, restaurants blaze, advertising signs, potted plants and washing lines elevate planners theory into people's reality. Sha Tin, for instance, designed for a population of five hundred thousand, is developing a truly metropolitan air. It is built on both sides of an artificially regulated waterway, and from the air, at least, it is possible already to see it as one of the great cities of the east. Dense high-rise clusters mark the city centre, a series of bridges cross the waterway, there are parks and plazas and waterside walks and a racecourse; and as if to cap the town's ideological progress, at its southern end there stands an immense new private residential estate called City One — fifty-two concrete towers, twenty-seven to thirty-four storeys high, attended by gardens, swimming pools and shopping plazas, and inhabited by one hundred thousand upwardly mobile Chinese families, each with a car in its carport — allegorical children of the refugees, living in allegorical buildings.

97

Glitz, Gusto and Exuberant Enterprise

In a celebrated tour de force, the Englishman Sir Norman Foster conceived the Hongkong and Shanghai Bank, the first truly advanced building, by world standards, to go up in Hong Kong. The grey-clad steel structure is the fourth of the bank's headquarters to occupy the same site, overlooking Statue Square with an unobstructed view of the harbour. Adjacent, the salmon-pink granite tower of the Chartered Bank rises a few feet taller in a typical Hong Kongism statement.

$\mathbf{S}$o two dramatically disparate urges, the urge to make money and the urge to relieve suffering, have created contemporary Hong Kong. By normal standards no one could call it architecturally beautiful. Random and sprawling as it is, in what appears nowadays to be a perpetual state of flux, demolition and construction, hideously overcrowded, restless and overheated, sometimes it seems altogether out of control. Yet somehow the whole adds up, matter and spirit blending, to a thing of paradoxical majesty. No city expresses more frankly, more fascinatingly or perhaps more disturbingly the elemental vigour of mankind.

One might suppose that in the uncertain last years of colonial status, the building of Hong Kong might be in hiatus. In fact unforseeable architectural postscripts are now being written. On the one hand, for the first time the government is concerning itself with the preservation of historic buildings, so that some of the surviving Manchu monuments are being snatched from ignominy or oblivion. On the other hand, as a more cosmopolitan capitalism has moved into Hong Kong in the wake of the retreating British Empire, bringing with it notions and values from around the world, individual buildings have arisen out of an altogether fresh daring and originality.

One after the other these great structures have appeared, each more showily publicized than the one before. Not all of them, of course, are distinguished, and all too many of them are characterized by an instinct for gigantism, in the Roman or for that matter the old Chinese style. Immense atriums are *de rigueur*, vast columns of coloured marble (specially imported from Italy, very likely), monumental staircases, effects of space or masonry that look like cathedral chancels, or bits of the Great Wall. To be bigger than the building next door is a prime object of construction, and best of all is to be the biggest in Asia, or even in the world. The general scale of things is swollen and vulgar; the architectural forms are newly aggressive.

But few of them are *boring*. No self-respecting Hong Kong entrepreneur would now build in the old mock-Mies, box-of-bricks, curtain-wall monotony, and the new willingness to deal in unexpected shapes and textures, while it sometimes seems mere exhibitionism, nevertheless expresses Hong Kong's saving grace of flexibility far better than the old orthodoxies did. I don't think feng shui concerns itself much with the actual appearance of buildings, but I think its practitioners would approve of this architectural profligacy anyway, as being properly in keeping with the setting, the spirit and the history of Hong Kong.

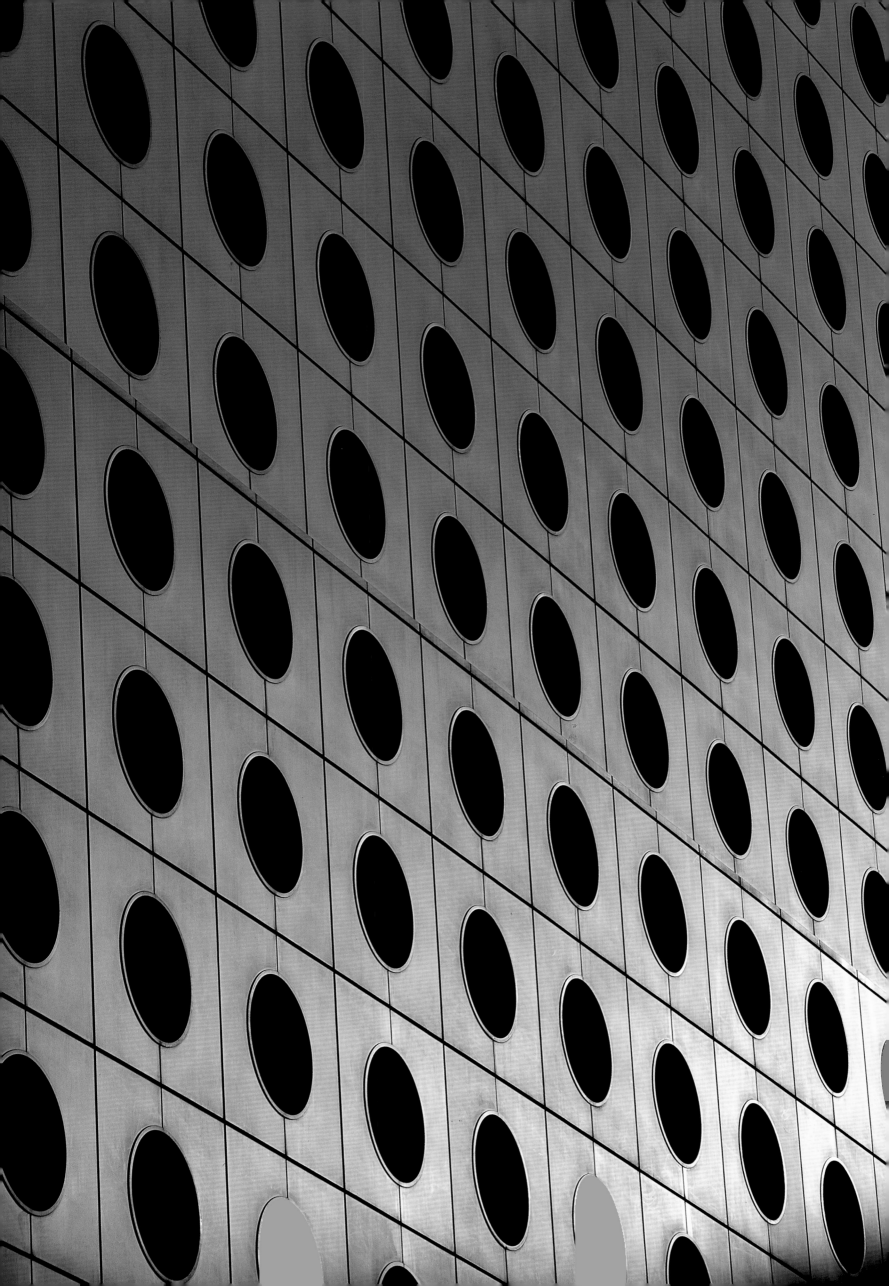

Connaught Centre, now Jardine House, was the first of a new breed of architectural statements on Hong Kong's skyline. Built by Jardine Matheson & Co, the building, designed by the venerable firm of Palmer and Turner, created an architectural revolution in the early 70s. (Previous pages) Pacific Place, a "city within a city", spacious by any standards, was designed by Jackson Wong of Wong & Ou Yang. It comprises of three five-star skyscraper hotels and an office tower above an enormous shopping mall complex with cinemas.

A New Breed

The first of the new breed was the Connaught Centre, now Jardine House, a semi-skyscraper covered all over with so many circular orifices that it immediately attracted a number of indelicate nicknames. It has long been succeeded by dozens of buildings at least as striking, some of them grouped in powerful clusters, some all on their own. The seventy-eight-storey Central Plaza, for a time the tallest building in Asia, is triangular in shape, Augustan in manner, and illuminated by baffling sequences of coloured lights, elucidated for curious visitors by printed schedules available at the reception desk. The Far East Exchange is sheathed in gold and is affectionately known as the Amah's Tooth. The Macau Ferry Terminal houses not only futuristic docks for hydrofoils, jet-foils and hovercraft, but a hotel, a shopping centre and offices, all contained within a package of slick and for my tastes highly invigorating trendiness. The Times Square complex is served by semicircular escalators, like the grand staircases of European palaces. The Cultural Centre on the Kowloon waterfront looks like a pair of gigantic ski jumps, has the ironic distinction of ignoring altogether the magnificent harbour prospect, there being no windows on its southern side, and is relieved only by the clock tower of the Kowloon Railway Station, all that is left of the once momentous terminal.

The nearby Regent Hotel, on the other hand, splendidly exploits one of the best hotel sites on earth with a humped pile of marble and glass above a waterfront promenade; while its neighbour, The Peninsula, one of the *grande dames* of Asian hotels, has transformed its familiar but long-dwarfed original premises by adding a defiantly contemporary tower block, giving its guests harbour views again. The Coliseum concert hall is like an enormous square cooking dish, the Hong Kong Stadium has high roof arches of transparent fibreglass, and looks like some sort of seashell. The Convention and Exhibition Centre, beside the water in Wanchai, suggests to me a last consummation of the dockside warehouse, with a lavish

107

garden on its roof and two luxury hotels in sentinel behind. Pacific Place includes three five-star skyscraper hotels, cheek by jowl, above an enormous shopping centre, and beside it is the new Hong Kong Park, complete with a vaulted stainless steel aviary, a multilayered conservatory, a lookout tower and a Greek theatre. The dear old Repulse Bay Hotel, beloved by generations of empire builders, has been replaced by a mammoth apartment block with a square hole through it halfway up, Miami style, or perhaps with a bow towards La Défense in Paris; but at its foot a delicately contrived replica of the old restaurant does its best to honour the spirit of the place.

Place of Pilgrimage

Some internationally eminent practitioners have contributed to all this, and made the territory something of a place of pilgrimage for students of architecture. The Hong Kong virtuoso Simon Kwan, having made his name with the elegant Academy for the Performing Arts on the Central waterfront, has gone on to design a complete new university, the University of Science and Technology in the New Territories, which spills in a cool profusion down a hillside above the sea; with its spacious circular plaza, its David Hockney like decor of palms and tiling, its startling exploitation of curtain walls and girders, this seems to me a true foretaste of 21st-century academe. The Swiss Remo Riva has designed many Hong Kong buildings. Exchange Square, the glittering curvilinear complex which houses the Stock Exchange, is elegantly modernist in manner, but two more recent buildings represent a step sideways: the new headquarters of the Chartered Bank, in Statue Square, is a somewhat gaunt sort of elongated ziggurat, notable for its stained-glass windows, while the intriguingly post-modern Entertainment Building looks vaguely ecclesiastical, buttressed with a device that gracefully responds to the Gothic Anglican cathedral along the road. Harry Seidler of Australia designed the Hong Kong Club in Statue Square,

replacing the headily Victorian old clubhouse with a coolly linear exercise in restraint. The little balcony above the main entrance, looking down to the Cenotaph, is popularly supposed to be provided for the General Secretary of the Chinese Communist Party, when he reviews the takeover parade in 1997. The Chinese-American I.M. Pei designed, in an appropriately declarative mode, the seventy-storey Bank Of China, Beijing's prime statement of supremacy in Hong Kong, and the nearest the place has to an icon-building, like Sydney's Opera House or London's Tower Bridge. With its lopsided silhouette and crowning masts, thanks to postage stamps and tourist brochures, it is fast becoming one of the best-known architectural shapes in the world.

The Englishman Terry Farrell has devised a startling new complex high on the Peak, shaped symbolically like a huge Chinese ideogram and looking indeed not unlike a victory memorial. The American Paul Rudolph, one of the most influential of 20th-century architects, designed the Lippo Centre, whose towers have a jaggedly cabalistic, or perhaps Aztec look. And in a now celebrated *tour de force*, Englishman Sir Norman Foster conceived the Hongkong and Shanghai Bank building at the head of Statue Square, the fourth of the bank's head offices to occupy the same site.

This was the first truly advanced building, by world standards, to go up in Hong Kong, and though it has since been overtaken in astonishment by newer rivals, it remains to my mind the presiding masterpiece of the city — the last great architectural monument of the British Empire. Built of grey-clad steel, cast about with great cross-girders, it has an air of terrific audacity, very proper to its site in the heart of Central. It looks less like a building than a portentous machine, and indeed all its functions are bound together with hidden electronics, with subtle sequences of elevators and with escalators whose oblique slants were decreed by feng shui. In height the building is dwarfed by I.M. Pei's Bank of China, and the adjacent Chartered Bank, in a childish display

of Hong Kongism, was deliberately built a few feet taller; but in its strength and originality it unmistakably dominates the financial quarter of the city.

It has given momentum, too, to Hong Kong's happiest architectural phenomenon, the unexpected re-emergence of the old city centre, Victoria, as a civic focus of some splendour. So abruptly do things change in this mercurial metropolis that I have seen for myself all the ups and downs of fortune that have moulded Statue Square. When I first went to Hong Kong the piazza was still visually in its colonial prime — club, bank, court house and cricket field were still dominant, the plaza still fronted the water, and if Queen Victoria and her relatives had been removed (by the occupying Japanese during World War II), the stately Cenotaph had assumed their symbolisms. Thirty years later the worst had happened. The square had lost its cohesion, Hong Kong its ceremonial centre.

Look at it now, though, as we descend from our viewpoint on the Peak (travelling down on the same funicular, by the way, constructed with such pride by the Victorians a century ago, though now in modern Swiss-made rolling stock). The square seems smaller than it used to, but that is because the assemblage of great buildings that has arisen around it is of such remarkable presence. Some hulking, some towering, some sleek, some brutal, dressed in glass or gold or silver, these potent and interesting structures amount to an exhibition of late 20-century architecture. More importantly, they have made of Statue Square a true ensemble once more. Among them stands a grand survivor of Edwardian Hong Kong: Sir Aston Webb's former Supreme Court, now handsomely done up and turned into the Legislative Council building. With this old champion at their heart they have restored to the square its sense of focal consequence, and given back to colonial Hong Kong, just in time, a centrepiece worthy of its stature.

Epilogue

I suggested at the start of this book that by the nature of things the Hong Kong of the late 1990s must be the definitive Hong Kong, but as 1997 approaches there is certainly no sign of resignation. The new shapes of the city, all chunks and sharp angles and monolithic slabs, speak of an energy altogether unabated, and in fact so fierce is the momentum now that the very geography of Hong Kong is being shifted before our eyes. Tremendous land reclamations are drastically narrowing the harbour, and creating yet more sites for skyscraper developments. Familiar islets are being obliterated, or united with the mainland to be islets no more. One of the great new airports of the world is being built on the outlying island of Chek Lap Kok, to be linked with the centre by new roads and railways and a tremendous suspension bridge, and served by yet another new town. Huge developments of the port are altering entire districts. New highways, new tunnels, new office blocks, new housing estates, a myriad of new footbridges and crawling hillside escalators — wherever one looks, Hong Kong is more than ever in motion.

It is in the nature of a historical fulfilment that, at the conclusion of one hundred and fifty years of phenomenal success, definitive Hong Kong should build itself out with all its old greed, gusto and exuberance.

Trefan Morys, 1995

Caught in the rays of a setting sun, the seventy-eight-storey Central Plaza, for a time the tallest building in Asia, designed by Dennis Lau & Ng Chun Mun, towers over the Hong Kong Exhibition and Convention Centre, designed by the same team of architects. (Previous pages) Black Italian marble underscores the cool elegance of the Grand Hyatt's lobby, designed by Hirsch Bedner and Associates.